YOUR KNOWLEDGE HAS VALUE

Bibliographic information published by the German National Library:

The German National Library lists this publication in the National Bibliography; detailed bibliographic data are available on the Internet at http://dnb.dnb.de .

Imprint:

Copyright © 2019 GRIN Verlag
Print and binding: Books on Demand GmbH, Norderstedt Germany
ISBN: 9783346023070

This book at GRIN:

https://www.grin.com/document/498967

Mohamad Ali Mohamad

Startup Enterprises in the Field of Digital Products in Germany and the United States. What is the Difference?

GRIN Verlag

GRIN - Your knowledge has value

Since its foundation in 1998, GRIN has specialized in publishing academic texts by students, college teachers and other academics as e-book and printed book. The website www.grin.com is an ideal platform for presenting term papers, final papers, scientific essays, dissertations and specialist books.

Visit us on the internet:

http://www.grin.com/

http://www.facebook.com/grincom

http://www.twitter.com/grin_com

THE DIFFERENCES BETWEEN STARTUP ENTERPRISES IN THE FIELD OF DIGITAL PRODUCTS IN GERMANY AND THE U.S.

.

Mohamad Ali Mohamad

Contents

1.Introduction

The terms startup and entrepreneurship are on everyone's lips. There is the talk of digitalization and a new world to be created by innovatively driven start-ups. Since I am in the process of starting my startup and am in this new economic world, I want to find out the secrets of the most successful companies in the world. GAFA, a term known in the inner circle of the Startup Community. The name is composed of the first letters of the four best known and most successful former startups in the world. Google, Amazon, Facebook, and Apple. If you look at all four companies, you will find some similarities, and it seems as if there is a draft, a basic framework on which all the companies mentioned are based. I've been looking for this framework for a year now and this way I notice again and again that there is no framework, but rather a law of nature that distinguishes successful startups from not so successful ones.

Nevertheless, some similarities can be observed. All GAFA companies come from the land of dreams, from the area where everyone can achieve everything. Google, Amazon, Facebook, and Apple all come from the United States. This commonality suggests that the corporate environment is a variable that can determine success and failure. In the following I would like to compare the conditions for startup companies between Germany and the United States of America and find out why no other German startup on the level of GAFA companies has made it since April 1, 1972 (founding year of the largest European software manufacturer from Germany: SAP). This question can be answered using the ecosystem of the two countries. Here I refer to some scientific research and to some perceptions of startup enthusiasts who could smell the startup air of both states. I can examine the differences between the three levels. On the one hand, there are the external conditions that affect startups, these cannot be controlled or changed by the startup itself. On the other side, there are the internal conditions that affect startups; these can and are controlled by the startup itself. Another analysis point is the support system, which can have a significant influence on how a startup develops.

2.External conditions influencing startup companies

As described above, external conditions are factors that cannot be controlled or influenced by the company itself.[1]

a)Legal basis and bureaucratic effort:

If you compare the steps you have to take to set up a company in the two countries, there are no real differences.[2] However, it should be borne in mind that the infrastructure in the United States is more digitized and therefore less bureaucratic. In some regions of the United States, for example, there are online services that make it possible to set up a business from home, while in Germany you first have to contact various offices to finally conclude the process with the notary.[3]

b)Various accesses for startups:

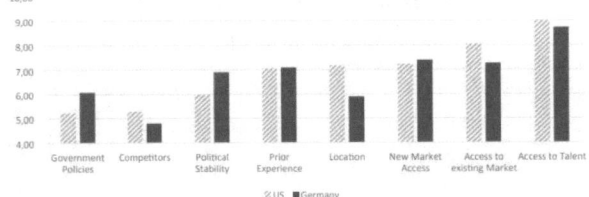

Figure 5. Detailed score of importance of different external factors

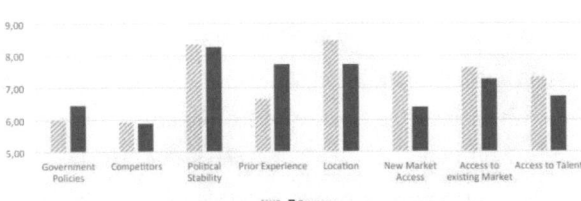

Figure 6. Detailed score of favorability/satisfaction of different external factors

Another difference can be seen in access to new talents and recruitment. One of the most important conditions that the United States has are the many elite universities. Harvard, MIT and Stanford University graduates are available to

---

[1]The startup ecosystems in Germany and in the USA. Explorative analysis and comparison of the startup environments - Conference: 5th Annual International Conference on Innovation and Entrepreneurship (IE 2015), At Singapore, Volume: Five. Zugriff am 02. März.2019

[2] Learn4Good. How to Start a Business / Company in the United States. Zugriff am 04.März.2019 & fuer-gruender. Mit welchen Gründungskosten und welcher Gründungsdauer Sie bei einer GmbH-Gründung rechnen müssen. Zugriff am 03.März.2019

[3] Same sources as point 3

an American start-up. Not only the high educational level of the graduates makes the difference, but also the internationality. A startup must act and react quickly. Startup companies, therefore, need easy access to new and old markets. This condition is better in the United States than in Germany. It can be seen that while access to new markets is essential for all start-up companies surveyed, it does not meet expectations in Germany.[4]

c)Education in the field of Entrepreneurial Action and Thinking:

Education is the highest resource humanity has and education is ideally passed on through schools, but unfortunately not when it comes to entrepreneurship. I can say from experience that most of my classmates don't even know what a company is and how it can work. The term startup has never been used in any subject in school, and that makes a huge difference. If you look at the Global Entrepreneurship Monitor (GEM), you see that Germany is far behind the United States when it comes to entrepreneurship education in schools.[5]

UNTERNEHMERISCHE BILDUNG AN SCHULEN

Rang	Land	Wert 1	Mittelwert 3.2	6
1	Netherlands	5.6		
2	Indonesia	5.1		
3	United Arab Emirates	5.0		
4	Estonia	5.0		
5	Lebanon	4.8		
6	Qatar	4.3		
7	Latvia	4.3		
8	Sweden	4.1		
9	USA	4.0		
⋮	⋮ ⋮	⋮		
39	Japan	2.7		
40	Argentina	2.6		
41	Mexico	2.6		
42	Germany	2.6		
43	Chile	2.5		
44	Panama	2.5		

Quelle: Global Entrepreneurship Monitor, Global Report 2017/18

---

[4] The startup ecosystems in Germany and in the USA. Explorative analysis and comparison of the startup environments - Conference: 5th Annual International Conference on Innovation and Entrepreneurship (IE 2015), At Singapore, Volume: Five. Zugriff am 02. März.2019

[5] Rkw-kompetenzzentrum. Global Entrepreneurship Monitor 2017/2018. Zugriff am 05. März. 2019

3.Internal conditions affecting startup companies

As described above, internal conditions are factors that are controlled and governed by the company itself.

In general, the focus of internal factors of german startups and american startups on entirely different levels. While American startup companies focus on the team, a work culture that fits the company's vision and the right co-founder, German startup companies focus on the product, marketing strategy and ability to scale[6]. Some conclusions can be drawn from these findings. American startup companies first build a foundation and then take care of the product. From the experience of my own start-up company, I can say that the product will change over time. That's how it's been on Facebook, Google, Amazon, and Apple, and it will always be the same. If the startup company doesn't have a strong foundation, it can't withstand these changes. At the beginning of every startup company you have a vision, this vision is the compass and the heart of the company, but the vision is not static, but always flexible. As a start-up company, you need employees who harmonize with each other and survive these rapid visions of change. But if you do it like in Germany and concentrate only on the product, the marketing, and the scalability, no working culture can be created and therefore no strong harmonizing team.

a)The meaning of the co-founder:

My mentor Arian Ney explained this to me as follows; the co-founder search is just like the marriage partner search, only more complicated. Not only must they trust each other blindly, but they must also complement each other. These hurdles are essential for the further development of the start-up company. The co-founders complement each other, respect each other, yet they question each

---

[6] The startup ecosystems in Germany and in the USA. Explorative analysis and comparison of the startup environments - Conference: 5th Annual International Conference on Innovation and Entrepreneurship (IE 2015), At Singapore, Volume: Five. Zugriff am 02. März.2019

other at the same moment. This mixture must be perfectly coordinated. Otherwise, it cannot work, because if there is no water in the spring, you cannot expect a lake at the end.

b)Why work culture can decide the life and death of a startup

The work culture in a start-up company includes various aspects. It's about internal written principles and even the working environment or why did you think Google inside looked ike a children's playground?[7]

The primary objective of such a working culture is to provide a guide for the participants to maintain the vision. Most companies try to achieve a stronger connection between the participants and the company.

For example, a definition of the work culture at Google could look like this.

Google

Problem: The world's information is disorganized and out of reach.
Vision: To provide access to the world's information in one click.
Mission: To organize the world's information and make it universally accessible/useful.
Principles: Focus on the user and all else will follow, it's best to do one thing really, really well, fast is better than slow, democracy on the web works, you don't need to be at your desk to need an answer, you can make money without

---

[7] Forbes.(Aug 29, 2018) How To Create A Positive Workplace Culture. Zugriff am 05. März. 2019

doing evil, there's always more information out there, the need for information crosses all borders, you can be serious without a suit, great just isn't good enough.

4.Supporting forces for startups:

Supporting forces for a startup company are one of the most important, if not the most critical condition that can exist in a startup ecosystem. Supporting forces are mostly incubators and accelerator programs. These try to promote startups in your region through various offers. Offers are on the one hand offering a workspace, mostly in open-plan offices, in a so-called co-working space, providing a network to other startups, experts and investors. If you look at the extent to which incubators and accelerator programs are relevant for

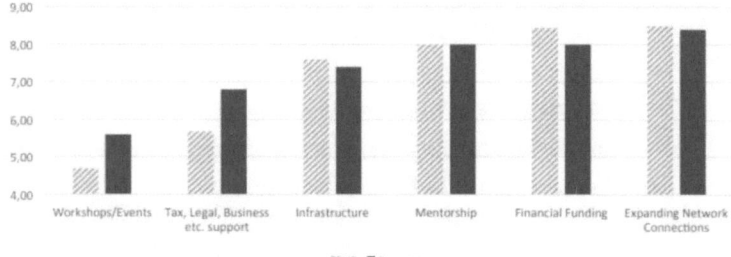

Figure 7 Detailed score of importance of support from Incubator/Accelerator

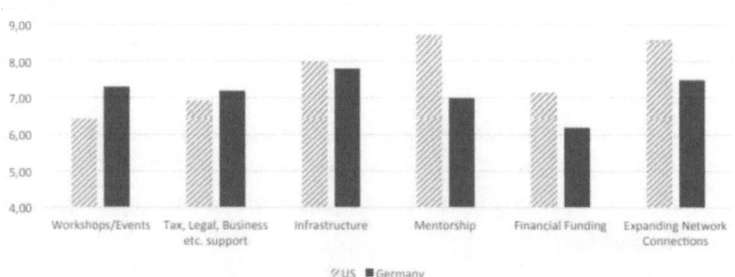

Figure 8. Detailed score of favorability/satisfaction of support from Incubator/Accelerator

startups, similar needs can be identified. However, it can also be seen that the

Us American startup companies are more satisfied in the area of financing opportunities and mentorship.[8]

a)Expanding Network Connections

Another significant aspect which can decide whether a startup will be successful or not is that network. My mentor Arian Ney taught me that my network is my most significant currency in the whole process. Because only those who have a wide-ranging network filled with experts can master the problems or questions of their start-up company, a market-specific network can also help to get to know the market better and help with product development. Looking at the above statistics, it can be seen that although both parties assess the importance of the network equally, it is also the case that the German startup companies are not satisfied according to expectations.[9]

b)Mentorship

In addition to an extraordinarily broad network, mentorship is one of the most critical aspects that exist. Mentorship for startup companies serves to protect you from the problems and hurdles that every startup will face. Ideally, it is for startup companies to have access to mentors through the Regional Incubators and Accelerator Programs. If these are not widespread in the region, as in my case, one has to procure mentorship for oneself via the Internet laboriously. As you can see from the statistics, both sides know the importance of mentorship the same, but you can also see that the American startup companies are more satisfied in the perception that the German startup companies[10].

---

[8] The startup ecosystems in Germany and in the USA. Explorative analysis and comparison of the startup environments - Conference: 5th Annual International Conference on Innovation and Entrepreneurship (IE 2015), At Singapore, Volume: Five. Zugriff am 02. März.2019

[9] Same source as point 8

[10] Same source as point 8

c)Financial Funding

No matter how good a Startup Ecosystem may be, no matter how good the network and no matter how good the incubators are, if Startup companies don't get money, they can't grow and are doomed to fail. As you can see from the statistics, the financial component is crucial for both German and American startup companies, but you can also see that the expectations and satisfaction of both parties are lower, whereby you can also see that the American startup companies have a higher score than the German startup companies[11]. From experience, I can say that it is complicated to get investors in Germany to finance start-ups in the initial phase. The mentality counts just as much as the school system for the students, which keeps security in the first place; it is the same for the German investors. Usually, investments are only made when the start-up company generates sales, and the product is sufficiently developed to market maturity.

5.Conclusion:

In summary, I can say that the differences between German and American start-up companies are shaped by mentality and way of thinking. It is difficult to answer to what percentage the environment plays a role in the success of a start-up company and to what extent it can be changed. It should be noted, however, that Germans still have a lot to learn from the land of dreams. Favorable conditions such as larger markets, better access to new talents and the better supporting forces make a difference whether a start-up company is made in Germany or the USA.

6.Who is Arian Ney?

Arian Ney is a 23-years old impact-driven entrepreneur, who has collectively motivated and inspired hundreds of thousands of people. He got featured in

---

[11] The startup ecosystems in Germany and in the USA. Explorative analysis and comparison of the startup environments - Conference: 5th Annual International Conference on Innovation and Entrepreneurship (IE 2015), At Singapore, Volume: Five. Zugriff am 02. März.2019

numerous international publications including Entrepreneur Magazine, BuzzFeed, MyComeUp, etc. and is described as a "marketing sensation" and "the future you need to know". He is the co-founder and CEO of AVONEMEDIA, a social media powerhouse based in Berlin, Germany.

7.Source Directory:

Researchgate (December 2015). The startup ecosystems in Germany and in the USA. Explorative analysis and comparison of the startup environments - Conference: 5th Annual International Conference on Innovation and Entrepreneurship (IE 2015), At Singapore, Volume: Five. Zugriff am 02. März.2019

Verfügbar unter:
https://www.researchgate.net/publication/281406950_The_startup_ecosystems_in_Germany_and_in_the_USA_Explorative_analysis_and_comparison_of_the_startup_environments

Learn4Good. How to Start a Business / Company in the United States. Zugriff am 04.März.2019

Verfügbar unter
https://www.learn4good.com/settingup-business/starting-a-company-in-usa.htm

www.fuer-gruender.de. Mit welchen Gründungskosten und welcher Gründungsdauer Sie bei einer GmbH-Gründung rechnen müssen. Zugriff am 03.März.2019

Verfügbar unter:
https://www.fuer-gruender.de/wissen/unternehmen-gruenden/unternehmensformen/gruendungskosten-gruendungsdauer-gmbh/

Rkw-kompetenzzentrum. Global Entrepreneurship Monitor 2017/2018. Zugriff am 05. März. 2019

Verfügbar unter:
https://www.rkw-kompetenzzentrum.de/gruendung/studie/global-entrepreneurship-monitor-20172018/

Forbes.(Aug 29, 2018) How To Create A Positive Workplace Culture. Zugriff am 05. März. 2019

Verfügbar unter:

https://www.forbes.com/sites/pragyaagarwaleurope/2018/08/29/how-to-create-a-positive-work-place-culture/#1daf9d8f4272